Beautifully Scarred

A Book of Freedom

By Savanah Graham

Inspired by my wonderful, patient spirit guides,

my beautiful, accepting animals, unconditionally loving angels, on this earth and above,

and the soul-moving places we have been blessed to experience together.

Thank you for this second chance of life, and the words to give breath to the flame that shall bring light to the ones still in darkness.

Awakening

The journey is not easy. The destination is unknown. Yet, every day I am more certain of the reasons my soul chose to embark on this earth-walk of life.

To wake up each day thankful to have another chance to take every single experience as the opportunity to evolve spiritually into my higher self and into a better human being. To leave each person, each animal, each field of energy with a positive essence of love and acceptance.

To take each sign and coincidence as a blessing and reminder to have faith in the creation of my own existence. To use my journey as inspiration and hope to all I am blessed to share it with, as well as motivation to continually work towards the

re-alignment of my own spirit.

To breathe and trust the process.

To surrender resistance.

To welcome change,

and to never, ever stop fighting to create the most magnificent life for all.

For we are all connected,

and every single thing is happening for a reason.

Now, what are you living for?

May you rediscover your Wings.

May you be Free.

What is true freedom?

Your mind thinks it knows...

But as soon as it attempts to label it,

define it,

seek out a meaning for it...

Its truth is already lost.

For freedom is not something you can describe,

achieve,

construct...

It is simply an awareness,

a state of being,

free.

****

My mind used to think that freedom was a place.

Nothing but limitless skies, breathtaking sunsets,

galaxies of stars...

Untouched by city lights,

unscathed by the trials of man,

the noise of human, frantic life...

Freedom to me was an endless trail through painted aspens. Brilliant snow against the silence of pine.

Mountains that grazed the surface of heaven with fingertips as delicate as they were jagged.

The mortal stairways to the endless playgrounds of the angels...

Freedom to me was foreign cathedrals, skeletons left to honor the magnificent, ethereal wonder surrounding their foundations.

Ancient places where the prayers still linger in the energy echoing off of the crafted stones, warmed in a sunset reflecting the thousands before.

Freedom to me was the map with no direction,
the compass with no needle,
the villages without names...
The true depth of an immeasurable, mystic forest
darkened with lore.
Mythical giants gripping a sacred earth with
their roots drawn inward.
To the place with no agenda, no expectations,
just simply the awesome and indescribable
knowing, resounding in your heart,
that this was all that was ever needed.

Freedom to me was the lake of sky.

Where abalone clouds became waves of liquid sunrise. The rose of dawn reflecting a sapphire twilight in its own glass of crystal.

Where the trees whisper in the breeze made by angel wings.

For it was they who painted the skies and made the waters dance in their visionary splendor.

Where desolation was peace, and the barren mountainsides were filled with their own native pulse. The tribal drumbeats in praise of the spectacular gift of life.

Freedom to me was the magic of the oceanside.

The lullabies the moon sang as her

mystery dipped below the horizon,

gently soothing the sand, still warm

from the sun.

Where the footprints were washed clean by the

tides slipping between jewels of sea shells

shimmering in their own explosion of diamonds,

illuminating a forgotten path.

No other place to be,

no schedule to follow,

breathing to the rhythmic pulse of the breaking

waves inside your soul.

Freedom to me was a mountain of solace.

Where the thunder rolls its power into the

chandelier skies of summer.

Where the rain becomes a child's heartbeat,

caressing every leaf as it falls into

the orchestra of the forest.

The trees with their leaves like stars

blessing the storm,

opening up without resistance, offering nothing

but love and gratitude.

When the mountain herself begins to sing,

and your own footsteps become the harmony to

the most instinctual song.

Freedom to me was a blanket of white,

cleansing the world in her pure, perfect silence.

The chance of renewal.

The chance of reflection.

To lay under her protection and quietly

remember what it truly is you came here to do.

When the earth is still

and you can hear the softest of snowflakes kiss

the ground. The purest recognition

and promise of heaven.

The most fragile exchange of hope.

The truest reminder that we are all unique and

flawless, coming to earth from a higher

perspective.

Our souls to awaken and kiss the same ground with the love from which they were created.

Only to grace this created realm with our own individual beauty.

Together as one,

to once again return home.

****

My mind used to think Freedom was a place.

*But freedom cannot be a destination.
It can only exist in the simple realization that we are nothing different from the snowflakes.
Freedom is being breath-taking and different, yet knowing no separation from the rest. Because we all are falling into this existence intending to be the purest examples of magic and rebirth.*

*For it is the essence of love to do so.
The same essence of love that created each of our souls to experience a reality reflecting its opposites.*

And so it shall forever be,

to the same essence of love that we will all once again return.

Freedom is love.

And it is our purest essence.

I would not be the snowflake I am today,

without my own incredible,

beautiful,

painful

fall back into awareness.

And it is now with more gratitude than I could ever describe, that I may begin to love every step that was and will be the adventure I am experiencing.

I hope that my journey and words resound in the deepest part of your own spirit, and awaken something within your own soul yearning to be remembered.

Because just as the scars are the body's reminder of awakening, memories are the souvenirs of the soul.

Both are beautiful,

both are love.

All it takes is the slightest shift of perception.

A Letter from Home

Wishes are whispered,

All dreams come true.

So once upon a time,

There was a little soul, who

Looked down from heaven,

And saw from afar

Two earth-bound souls

Both wishing to start.

Their own family,
Their creation of love
A child, an angel
On earth, from above.

And without doubt
The little soul knew,
That its purpose was clear
Beginning with these two.

So with a final glance
Of its sweet paradise,
It imagined a birth
To begin its earth life.

But a strange thing happens
When souls are reborn,
They forget their connection
From which they were formed.

So the soul got lost
Forgetting its path.
Among the judgment, the separation,
The ego's own wrath.

So cold was this earth,
So limited this shell.
That body, with mind
Could create their own hell.

Searching for escape
Through pain and high,
Anything to make
The suffering subside.

So for years it wandered,
In search of the light.
That it knew in its heart
Would bring peace to the night.

Teeming with worry
Made restless its strife.
Inviting fears to linger
Bringing demons to life.

So the little soul did,
The only thing it could do.
To escape the torment,
These humans made true.

By killing its vision
So scared and so sad,
Because the light of their souls
Forgot the bond it once had.

With the highest truth
Never separate from,
The love that unites
The stars and the sun.

With the forests of emerald
Speckled with gold.
In the melting sunlight
Where the secret is told.

That we are all united
In this sacred dance.
Every moment, every heartbeat,
Is its own second chance.

To once again live
In the purest of grace,
And remember the song
A soul yearns to create.

In hopes to ignite

The ancient spark

That begins the fire

To diminish the dark.

The dark where we hide,

Our flaws and our scars,

The skeletons dusted

With tears like stars.

Living in a lie

We are unworthy, unloved,

And everything sinned

Is punished from above.

But deep in its being
The quietest of places,
The little soul knew
The unconditional graces.

That flowed down from heaven
And straight to earth.
Giving its magic, its bliss
The promise of rebirth.

But how to convince
A world of hate
Of this unconditional love
Before it was too late?

So the little soul

Made a promise so deep.

That it would use what it learned

To awaken all from sleep,

And rise from their slumber

To remember their home.

And use the little soul's journey

To bring light to their own...

If I die today...
Please tell him how much I love him.

If these were my final moments among these trees, these mountains... This earth-plane where too much is said and not enough is felt. In this cold place where emotions have been replaced by symbols on a keyboard and too often are we left feeling empty and incomplete...

If this was my last day, as human, in this shell of body, worn and weathered by pain and challenge, tired by travel, the relentless search for purpose and reason.

The last day of suffering, the last day of seeking...

Then tell them I was a fighter.
That the trials I had chosen for myself before entering this life, were hard but not impossible.
Nothing is.

That every demon was self-created, and the only battle was conquering my own mind. Pain does not exist. It is only a reminder that what you have is never promised. Nothing except the present, fleeting moment is promised, and it is up to you to cherish every ounce of it with your entire soul.

It is ok to tell them my only happiness was in the forests. Among the mountains holding solid to the earth that once thrived without greed and war. Let them know I was never of this world. Its pre-set society and conceptualized reasons for what is "right" and "normal". Freedom was getting lost from the noise of ego, of material, and surrendering to everything primitive,

un-expected,

un-planned,

un-scheduled and un-known. I was a fighter because I was born into a place trying only to control my mind, a place where if it wins, you lose your soul until this day, like mine, where its last few physical breaths are taken.

Tell them I left because my time in this realm had served its purpose, only to compliment the purpose of me leaving it.

Tell them I was grateful for every single moment.

And that we are all immortal,

We can never be hurt.

You Must First Let Go of the Past

How many times

Must one world burn

To only begin anew?

When the ashes of past silently fall,

To earth still shining with dew?

When the sunlight fades
Through clouds of smoke
That once were clouds of rain.
That bore the promise of rebirth
And not the promise of pain.
When the sparks ignite
The flame bears girth
Against the stormy seas.

The ocean of dreams

Thought once of wealth

Only cry waves that bleed.

To the higher snows

Our hopes arose

When the tide it changed once more.

But the white of ash

Was all that fell

To the wreckage against the shore.

You left me silent,

Amidst the bones

Had died our saving grace.

The broken hearts,

The empty soul,

The rage you threatened I face.

Starved for love,

I fell once more

To the arms that beckoned true

But in midnight moon

I'd slip away soon

And hunt for sleep anew.

The frigid cold

I dared to save

A sanity clung to grasp.

The lonely souls

To malice slope

Your warmth would be my last.

I fought to save

The bitter piece

Of what was left of mine.

But winter's keep

Soared quickly steep

Thus drowned in its decline.

The wall of strength

Left crumbling dust
The dream that fueled the flame.
Now broken soul
An eminence dull
Of a life it mirrored the same.
But in the sand
Was buried hope
And once again I flew.
To the haven saved
In the mountains made
For healing the flesh
Starved blue.
The beauty there found
Like Tanager sound
The surprise of discovery gold.
A sleepless night
Of pure delight

Held hope in promises told.

Once more a careful wall was built

To save the precious dove.

A life of those,

A thriving rose,

Two souls met far above.

A depth of truth

Coursing through

A river carried free.

The songs of future

Bliss and sky

Two spirits meant to be.

But in the perfect air of night,

It was a breath

That caught the flame.

A butterfly wing

Of gold they sing

Flickered just the same.
The indigo depths
Of empty loss
Danced across the floor.
Following lead
Of gasoline
Laid down the night before.
The skies they cried
With your goodbye
The glass like shattered rain.
The walls to sand
Once more to hand
Over the price of pain.
The fire rose
Like passion lost
In the hollow caves of heart
Where flames, they licked

The granite walls
Where dreams where torn apart.
Once more a world
Built by love
Destroyed with claws of fate
The crushing wall
Of tide once more
A spirit free to break.
You promised a life
I dreamed before
And knew it once
As true.
But by angel eyes
My soul did cry
For it was she
You gave it to.

An Eagle Made Golden

How do I tell them that I am not of this place, and my journey inside the realm of the angels is one I must do alone? How do I explain the absence of physical attachment, the absence of a material experience for which I yearn?

How can I tell them how much I love them, but only in the reality of their true souls and spiritual development? How may I make them understand that we are all growing together and how crucial it is that our connection is used to learn, and not control? To strive for complete, unrestricted acceptance, but not to resist the experiences given to us in which to practice it? How to even begin to tell the truth of the unconditional love that exists to make us limitless as souls when the human ears have forgotten how to listen to the stars?

Vida

Just as the ancient gods craved the life of mortals, we as our own creators of freedom yearn to leave the confines of our captured heaven. Daring to slip past its golden boundaries to touch the foreign waters of this spiritual life. I know one day I will understand the reasons behind the suffering and the battles fought on this trodden ground above, but for the moment I feel the tragic in my heart. Silent sleeps the souls in the hills beside me as the physical strife burdens deep into the bonds I thought once unbreakable.

"Patience my child",

I listen,

"There is love far greater than what you are fighting for. Have faith and give breath to the life you yourself chose to define and to learn. Find yourself and be love."

Avalanche Lake

Since the day she left that place
She would close her eyes,
And dream of the peaks
Reflecting grace
Whispering to the skies.

Weightless their waters
She made into glaciers,
Crystal green, were their emerald dyes.

That she painted the walls
Built up around her.
With sapphire thunder,
In silent goodbyes.

That echoed against
The miles that kept her
From feeling the freedom
Where the last tears had dried.

But the promise she made there
She still carries with her
And still it resounds
Against the pines.

That keep sacred the shore
She will picture once more
The place where her heart aligns.

Reflection

We wouldn't be scared
If we couldn't feel the potential.

We wouldn't hold back
If we didn't know.

We wouldn't hide
Or dance beside
The truth that our eyes both show,

If it wasn't real.

Our nerves wouldn't be still,
If we couldn't feel the power.

Our pulse wouldn't race
If we didn't think forever.

We couldn't hide
Or hold inside
The love that only gets better.

I promised you words
And with it my heart
I give you this life a day to start
Something beautiful...

Because, everything you imagine is real.

Leaves like Stars

Its roots spread

Beneath the water,

The branches a galaxy

And the stars fell like rain.

Making the reflection ripple

Of the tree you once thought was real.

March 6

To all my black sheep,

the trespassers... the ugly ducklings... the non-conformists... the rebels... the tattooed, the crazy, the wicked, the skeptics, the open-minded, the thinkers... the restless, the wild... the broken-hearted and thick-walled, heavily guarded truth seekers, the hopeless romantics, the poets... the artists, the daring, the courageous and independent, the defiant, the outlaws.. the fire-starters and rule-breakers, the adrenaline junkies, the pyros and star-counters... the dream-catchers and sunset-chasers... the impulsive, relentless, fearless, creative, luminous lovers of freedom...

Don't ever stop.

For we exist in a world of fear-based tyrants,

yet we dare to live a life based on love.

For it was from love which we were created,

As pure spirits to experience our true freedom of will.

It is we who are not afraid,

and it is we who are destined to remind the rest.

And The Rain Brings Heaven Closer

This morning you gave me,

A magic unreal...

When I stopped at the crest

Of the stairs made stone,

I prayed for a sign

That I was not alone.

The wind it howled

Through the trees now bare.

Clouds so low, so close the air.

Like wings that brushed

Against my skin.

The trees they danced

To the calling wind.

Such gray a sky

Could only foresee

The sunrise of gold

That was to be.

But not until

I stopped once more

Did the rays of light

Hold on no more.

To the cloud's confines,

Of silent gray,

Breaking through a world

Covered in shade.

I could not grasp
My emotions too deep.
This heaven on earth
A dream without sleep.

No body's wall
Nor trying sight,
Could capture the magic
That had escaped the night.

My soul it danced
In the shimmering light.
Catching fire the trees
That circled my flight.

Now with the wind
Soaring through the sky.
Its pieces of blue
Like an eagle's cry.

Brilliant and clear
Tore through the gray
That only before
Had cradled the day.

Fly for Me

I stopped and prayed just as the sunlight caught a chance to break away from the clouds, casting light to the intense, blue canvas behind the trembling pines, swaying in the frigid wind that against my closed eyes reminded me of bitter winter - the winter on the tops of mountains, where the air is like crystal and fills your lungs,

your soul,

with life.

I stopped there for a moment, taken back to that sacred place that drives my restless spirit. Silently thanking the pines, the sky, the wind, all for reminding me of what is greater, and higher, and all happening in natural reason... all flowing on the winding path to what is so tirelessly sought.

And in my quiet blessing, just as the years before, I watched my beautiful angel, my spirit hawk, catch the same wind from the pines and soar into the sun, promising that everything will be as it should.

Fly for me,
And watch over my soul.
In this life,
And into the next.

Dreams of Drifting

A ship with no sails
To the whim of the waves,
Crashing into the bow
Commandeered that day.
New to the hands,
Of those without plan
A compass due north
A journey began.
Where maps don't exist
And mystery prevails,
This daring adventure
A ship with no sails.
Somewhere in darkness
The island, it sleeps
Where the trees bear fruit

That both shall seek.
Without stars to light,
The snow it guides
Only into the wind
That tears at the sides.
To the ship afloat
In a hurricane's dance,
With no sails to protect
Their precious chance.
The course they travel
Thoughts stolen from dreams,
That once built barriers
To their faces unseen.
But on this ship,
There are no walls
No masks to disguise
The beautiful flaws.

A bare reality

The sand in the sun,

Of this future port

One day to become,

More than just

A fleeting glance

Into the dream

Needing only the chance.

<u>*February 2, 2012 at 5:03pm*</u>

Addicted solely to the adrenaline of survival... The reason for the reckless decisions painting the story of my life. Only when I am trapped in the monotony of daily routine do I fall, relentless are the demons I try so desperately to escape, the thoughts that keep my dreams from my sleep. It is the reason that fuels the pure electricity of my travels, the impulsive decisions to move, the lust for horizons yet unseen and sunsets secretly exploding the skies of another atmosphere... Somewhere I know, somewhere I have felt the warmth before... I crave that feeling of life, of living in mystery and adventure and wanderlust... of freedom in the depths of unfathomable possibilities, to feel the breath of the wings that cradle my dreams and the wind from the skies that reflect into the glass of reality that so beautifully shatters, the moment you hold it close...

Mountain Rain

Patient be, my child.

For even the rain waits to fall.

Days of quiet

When the trees are still

And the sunlight fades into the chance of storm.

High in the heavens they wait

For their chance to fly

To meet the ground,

To scale the trees,

To feel the pulse of earth...

To glisten in mornings,

And bring promise of life,

To make the waters dance,

And the mountains sing

Our lullabies to peace.

Patient now my little one

For the rain makes it true.

That even the waters

Made by angels

Must wait to meet their world anew.

Sometimes the winds lose us from ourselves,

From the world...

In hopes we find a newer place.

Where the footprints are strangers,

And our souls can grow.

It is the wheel that breaks the wings

That lay like stains of glass

A window to the universe never straying from its course.

Secrets hidden to truths we strive to remember...

The force that bounds us whole.

<u>Dear future self</u>...

*When you go back and find this day,
and these words,
I want to remind you how much I love you and how proud I am of you for doing the hardest and most painful thing you will probably ever have to do. Two nights ago you hit your lowest, crying in the arms of your mother on the cold kitchen floor... The reality of your life's sacrifice and purpose scattered around you like broken pieces of windows stained red,
but a reality only of transparent truth.
A window to a higher perspective that ultimately cascaded your world upside down. It was in those fragile hours that your soul slipped through the constellation of tears and gave itself rebirth. No longer could you accept the debt to be repaid manifested in your own mind.*

You owed him nothing. Yet for years you punished yourself for his own karmic creations...

It was only a reflection...

He left you because you abandoned yourself...

He ignored you and de-humanized you because you didn't love and accept yourself. It was you who ignored the crying, lost soul in the mirror. It was you who craved the thought of suicide because you had destroyed yourself inside. It was you, not him...

You owed yourself a happy and fulfilling life, not him. This is the reality that threw you to the hard, wooden floor because you finally sought the truth within your own self. This is the reality that broke the chains you bound yourself to him with. This is the reality that set you free.

So here you are.

One truck, one suitcase, two beautiful dogs, and the entire universe of creation.

Your angels are right beside you, your falcon always above you, and the pure, unconditional love you have always sought... Is always within you.

Sacred Dance

There is a tea cup

filled with ash,

of fire that burned

the memories past.

With the wax she melts

from the element's flame,

drawing black across

her cheek again.

To cover the ghosts

of tears she spent

the final day

her spirit wept.

The fire, it sinks

within her skin,

as the sweat of the wild

desires its sin.

Inside it claws

its way to life,

renounced,

reborn,

ancient wings take flight.

Aligned her spirit

it is once more,

from a fragile teacup,

a secret,

no more.

<u>Solace</u>

My Dearest Guardians, My Spirits, My Guides,
      I miss the days spent in the mountains so close to your energy.
The sunsets spent on the hillside, overlooking the perfect valleys in the glow of dusk.
How close you felt then, when all of my thoughts could rest on you.
I think I realize now, even in the human mind I seem to inhabit at the moment that you are but a breath away.
Your presence a mere vibration of pulsing energy higher, this veil slowly evaporating with every sunrise.

There is nothing that I think about as much as I do praying to see you, to feel you, to know for certain, as these two-dimensional senses require, that you are actually with me.

I know in my soul you are there always.

But I get so caught up in this human experience that I yearn for your physical validation, just as I yearn for the mountain peaks of Glacier. The only other place I felt truly home.

I miss you,

And I know I will see you soon.

I simply pray the signs you send will keep me at peace until we can finally embrace once more.

I trust you completely.

...And when I leave this earthen body,
I pray they will let me help you paint the sunsets

There is something immensely powerful in sunsets.
Something so pure
And so real,
That it gravitates your attention like a childhood memory craving warmth.
Something about the way the final rays of a star become so awesomely captivating, we named it our sun.
Integrated so closely, we call it one of our own.
As necessary as breath to life,
the same breath that ignites the fire within us all.
Maybe it is because the pure energy we raise our hearts towards is the same golden light that once created our soul.
Is that not what grips us then?

To become still and quiet, reflecting in the day's end, our own creation?

Is it the warmth of our true home, which we have forgotten as physical bodies, pulling to our inner spirits, rendering us speechless, motionless...

As we experience the subtle grace of the changing heavens of rose and sapphire?

Stunning in its illuminated trek across the flawless sky, to finally rest against the horizon. So close to our own beating hearts...

Just as every true love draws close,

Right before it disappears.

Only to rest in the arms of a promised tomorrow.

<u>Rest In Peace</u>

<u>My little lamb,</u>

<u>For fear was love</u>

<u>To return again.</u>

<u>Set free your soul,</u>

<u>Defy their lies,</u>

<u>And awaken a world,</u>

<u>Of Lions to Rise.</u>

The cold wraps its arms around me, beckoning like the familiar embrace of a worried parent.
It pulls me closer as the wind blows wisps of stardust, as snowflakes, into my breath.
Frozen.
Caught in the icy air.
Just like the golden rays of sunlight between the beckoning clouds.

Each step into the woods resting beautifully in white,

Everything dappled in mahogany browns and snow prints,

like a silent herd of painted ponies.

Still.

Waiting for the storm like me.

Deeper, the air grows quieter.

Only whispering the soft tread of frozen leaves beneath the settled snow.

Even the flurries become softer as I retrace a delicate trail long forgotten in the green of summer...

But now the masks are gone,

And the trees bare,

As they truly are.

Nothing is hidden when the first snow falls

And the camouflage of autumn is washed away clean by the honesty of winter.

...And so it was my purpose

As intricate and as perfect
As the seasons so dance.
I followed an instinct,
For it too was my chance.

To remove the colors,
Hiding my truth.
Just like the leaves,
Of a summertime's youth.

To finally fall,
From the highest of limb.
To surrender without fight,
For winter to begin.

Myself, a new season,

With nothing to hide.

And bring light to the pathways,

Where an ego had died.

Into a new realm

Where the snowflakes now fall.

Aligning once more

With my spirit's new call

To a winter, a freedom

Unlike anything known.

For when we've nothing to lose,

We are finally home.

As the stardust sings silently...

I would have spent the entire night
talking to the stars...
Because I know one day when we are together again, in that
beautiful in-between place, you will get to hear it, and know
I never gave up and kept you close.
Some days I wish I could leave this serrated earth, just so I
could hug your spirit.
I miss you more than you could possibly imagine.
Everywhere I go I take you with me, feeling in my heart that
we are once again experiencing this incredible life together.
Especially the twilights,
When I see the edges of my physical reality start to blur with
the sparks of the universe falling into my vision
like sequins from fireflies.
I can see the energy, it moves like excited stardust...

I just pray for the direction in which to send mine.

What do I do? Where do I go?

But that in itself seems frivolous when I cannot find a passion for this money-hungry, material founded world. No emotion. No attachment. I go through the movements only because it is necessary for me to do so.

For now.

While dreaming of the other worlds and higher-vibrational planes of existence that shimmer just above my limited perception.

How do I find the way to be present, and here, when all I can imagine is the comfort and love and understanding that is just beyond my grounded shell of a human body?

How do I find peace here?

When I am not of this world?

I spoke to the stars,

To you,

And sang our favorite songs from our memories of magic...

It was a freezing night, but I had made tea to hold and whiskey to warm my soul.

The sky was a flawless escape, each diamond glistening its perfection in the absence of any clouds.

Breathtaking in the endless obsidian.

I sang until the dreams came,

My earth angels, the whiskey for my heart.

We talked about you, until the night became the morning,

And our souls drifted into the blankets by the window full of stars.

May the Journey Continue

...Wishes are whispered,

All dreams come true.

So once upon a time,

There was a little soul, who

Dreamed of a life,

That no one could see.

With horizons unknown,

Undiscovered,

Set free.

A life that couldn't,

Be prisoned by bars.

That were made up of rules,

Set against the stars

Structured by time,

By appearance,

By age...

By status, by money,

By ego, this cage.

That everyone seemed,

Complacent to be

Kept in their lines,

By a sick society.

In fact they would even,

Challenge the light.

That shed truth on the greed,

Dissolving their flight.

Clipping their wings,

This illusion of fear.

That anything told differently,

They would refuse to hear.

"We must protect

What they say is right!

For we are powerless,

Unable,

Existing in fright!"

Of what could possibly

Be killing us all,

Of more pain, more suffering

We must struggle not to fall!"

"Because then what?!"

They cry,

"We go to hell!

Our souls condemned!

To be tortured

They tell!"

"So we all must follow,

What they preach to do!

Because God is vengeful

And will punish you!"

So they live in fear...

And not in Love.

Becoming the victims,

Each a wingless dove.

Because with their flight,

They surrender their faith,

In the paradise waiting

Where all souls are safe.

Faith in the truth,

That they simply forgot.

That life is the heaven,

We have tirelessly sought.

For our spirits know,

Deep within ourselves,

That the most beautiful of things...

Are not taken from shelves.

We cannot buy,

Our happiness craved.

Everything sought,

Is in the pure love that made,

Each and every,

One of us who,

Reflected the love,

Of a creator who knew.

That it could never experience

Every facet of life.

Without building the selfish,

The storms, the strife.

That wreak havoc upon,

The masses of souls.

Put through hell to experience,

What true heaven unfolds.

For heaven is simply,

The glance right through

The illusion of hell,

We make so true.

Because all it takes,

Is an act of grace

To re-align our spirits,

With our own creator's face.

For once we feel,

A choice love made.

We remember from where,

Our farewells were bade.

When we left our true home,

Amongst the stars

To be given the chance,

To break out of the bars.

And fight to help,

The rest remember.

That we were made to love,

And cherish another.

To change the illusion,

That we are all apart.

And love our differences,

With an open heart.

We are in this together,

This sacred chance to learn.

The unconditional love,

That our souls so yearn.

To feel without doubt,

That we are never alone.

And how we are all just walking

Each other back home.

And so it shall be

My restless soul always trying to capture the pure and magnificent snowflakes of magic, falling beautifully into this earth-realm from destinations more spectacular than can be described with my feeble, attempted human words...

Destinations so divine, so heavenly, it could only bless us with the most amazing reminders that we are not of this world, but of something so much greater and interconnected.

That every rainbow and flawless intimacy of wildflower is made of the same beautiful stardust crafted by an all-encompassing, unconditional love.

May I live every moment of this chance at life in boundless gratitude for these perfect reminders, fueling my hunger to remember and reflect this beautiful truth.

May we all live in such a quest, that every day be filled with wonder,

with magic,

And endless opportunities to be free in a world just waiting to be re-discovered.

For the path of rediscovery is not easy,

as life, it cannot be.

For without the darkness and scars,

how would we ever appreciate the beauty we have finally found?

Blessed be your own journey,

For mine is a continual gift that I am beyond blessed to share with you.

There are no Ends, only Beginnings

In dedication to the pure and beautiful soul of my unborn child.

May you always remember the truth of your limitless Freedom,

And feel in your heart, its complete, immortal acceptance of infinite, unconditional love.

This moment, and every moment,

until your first breaths are taken, with the first promise of snow.

And every beautiful moment, ever after.

Inspirations and Gratitude

The creation of this book was made possible not only by my amazing and insightful mother, and all other eyes and ears who read and critiqued its lines with an open heart, but by the incredible places I have been blessed on this journey to experience. Every poem and message was inspired by the indescribable emotions that penetrated my soul in these places of breath-taking splendor. It was the true, natural beauty that finally began to calm the restless spirit within my body's walls, deeply inside my soul it resonated with the unfaltering connection we share with all of creation. Therefore I would like to include the places that so captured my heart and enabled the words to flow through my thoughts and onto these pages. You can view/purchase my photographs of these captivating places in cadence with their inspired words on my website...

https://www.facebook.com/savanah.indigo

By following the link on my page for:

"Beautifully Scarred Ink."

Please feel free to contact me with your feedback, your questions and any part of your own journey you would like to share. I would savor the connection as we continue together to find light in the struggles and beauty in the scars!

Savanah Graham

733 Peaks St. Bedford VA 24523

Savanah21music@aim.com

Locations of Inspiration for Beautifully Scarred:

A Letter From Home and *The Rain Brings Heaven Closer* – Harkening Hill, The Peaks of Otter, Bedford, VA

You Must First Let go of The Past – South Lake Tahoe, CA Anchorage, AK. Blue Ridge Parkway, Bedford, VA

Vida – Jackson Hole, WY to Taos, NM

Avalanche Lake – Glacier National Park, MT

Leaves like Stars and *Mountain Rain* – Flat-top Trailhead, Peaks of Otter, Bedford, VA

March 6th and *As the Stardust Sings Silently* – Bedford, VA

Dreams of Drifting and *So it was my purpose* – Savage Mountain, MD

Dear Future Self and *Sacred Dance* – Frostburg, MD

Solace – Claytor Nature Center, Bedford, VA

<u>May you Rediscover your Wings, May you be Free</u> –

All places listed above, including the following:

Lake District, England, Playa Del Carmen, Mexico,

Black Forest, Germany, hidden vineyards in France,

Yosemite National Park, CA, Denali National Park, AK,

Desolation Wilderness, CA/NV, and all of the magical,

exhilarating places in between.

May your journey be ever beautiful...

Made in the USA
Charleston, SC
14 August 2014